BAKED

Delights

BAKED
Delights

LOVE FOOD™

This edition published by Parragon Books Ltd in 2014
LOVE FOOD is an imprint of Parragon Books Ltd

Parragon Books Ltd
Chartist House
15–17 Trim Street
Bath BA1 1HA, UK
www.parragon.com/lovefood

ISBN 978-1-4723-4181-5

Printed in China

Cover and internal design by Talking Design
New photography by Clive Streeter
New recipes by Angela Drake

Notes for the Reader

This book uses both metric and imperial measurements. Follow the same units of measurement throughout; do not mix metric and imperial. All spoon measurements are level: teaspoons are assumed to be 5 ml, and tablespoons are assumed to be 15 ml. Unless otherwise stated, milk is assumed to be full fat and eggs are medium.

Garnishes, decorations and serving suggestions are all optional and not necessarily included in the recipe ingredients or method. The times given are an approximate guide only. Preparation times differ according to the techniques used by different people and the cooking times may also vary from those given. Optional ingredients, variations or serving suggestions have not been included in the time calculations.

CONTENTS

INTRODUCTION

HOME BAKING IS MOVING ON – THE NEW BAKES ON THE BLOCK ARE FUN, FANCY, VISUALLY STUNNING, FULL OF FRESH FLAVOURS AND COMPLETELY DELICIOUS! FROM DELICATE ÉCLAIRS TO QUIRKY COOKIES, FASHIONABLE SWEETS AND SUPER STYLISH SMALL CAKES, THESE BAKED DELIGHTS ARE THE TALK OF THE TOWN!

Essential Equipment

Pop sticks – to make the Coconut Brownie Pie Pops (see page 36) and Chocolate Mint Cake Pops (see page 70), you'll need thin ovenproof lollipop sticks. You'll find them in most good kitchenware shops and department stores. They need to be about 15 cm/6 inches long.

Push pop containers – available to order online, these handy little reusable plastic containers are essential to make the Choc Chip Cookie Sundae Push Pops (see page 20). Simply fill and top with the lid then pop in the refrigerator until required. To eat, gently push up the stick to reveal the delicious contents inside.

Nozzles and piping bags – for piping macaroons and choux pastry, and decorating cupcakes and cookies, a selection of piping bags and various sized nozzles are essential. Make sure you have both a large plain and star-shaped nozzle as well as a variety of fine metal piping nozzles for intricate piping. Disposable plastic piping bags are a cheap and convenient alternative to a reusable piping bag.

Cookie cutters and templates – most bakers, even novices, will have a variety of round cookie cutters. But, if not, the rim of a glass can easily be substituted for stamping out circles of pastry

for pie pops or rounds of sponge for the mini ombre cakes. If you don't have a specific shaped cutter, simply draw and cut a template from card, trace around it onto baking paper, cut out and use as a guide. Ensure the card doesn't come into direct contact with food.

Cake tins and trays – along with the usual cake tins, muffin and cupcake trays, you'll need a couple of sturdy baking sheets for baking cookies, éclairs and macaroons. For the Piñata Party Cake (see page 22), two ovenproof mixing bowls are needed (or just one and bake half the mixture at a time). To make the classic oval-shaped friands (see page 72), look for a silicone mould online or just bake in a mini muffin tray.

Sugar thermometer – when boiling syrup for marshmallows and brittle, a sugar thermometer will take all the guess work out of the process and ensure perfect results every time. It will also come in handy to check the temperature of oil when deep-frying doughnuts.

Specialist Ingredients

All the recipes in the book are made with the usual baking ingredients – butter, sugar, eggs, flour, etc. As always, for the best tasting results, it's preferable to use the finest ingredients you can afford. Some recipes will require a few more specialist ingredients but most can be found in good cake decorating shops or can be ordered from the internet.

Food colourings – gel pastes or liquid colourings will give a good colour to cakes and icings, but be sure to add them gradually with a cocktail stick to achieve the desired colour.

Sugar sprinkles – sometimes called hundreds and thousands or funfetti, the world really is your oyster when it comes to sprinkles! Readily available from supermarkets, cake decorating shops or online, you can pick whichever colour combination or shape you desire!

Edible gold leaf – perfect for giving that touch of sophistication to the Salted Caramel Mini Éclairs (see page 38) buy sheets of gold leaf from cake decorating specialists. It's pricy and you only get a small amount, but just a little will give the desired effect. For a cheaper, but just as effective finish, dot the éclairs with tiny edible gold balls or sprinkle with edible gold glitter.

Cooking Techniques

Making choux pastry – there are a few golden rules to follow when making choux pastry. Only add enough of the beaten eggs to achieve a thick and shiny paste that drops from a spoon when tapped. Make sure the oven is at the correct temperature and sprinkle the baking sheets with a little water to help the éclairs rise. Don't be tempted to open the oven door too soon or the pastry may collapse and, finally, pierce the baked éclairs to allow any steam to escape and then return them to the oven for just a few minutes to ensure the pastry is crisp and dry.

Filling éclairs – to pipe filling into éclairs, use a large piping bag preferably fitted with a long piping nozzle. There's no need to split open the éclairs, instead, push the nozzle into a small hole at one end. Squeeze the filling in gently taking care not to overfill. For a quicker way to fill large éclairs, split them in half lengthways and drop small spoonfuls of whipped cream into the bottom halves.

Building a push pop – to fill push pops easily they need to be upright so it's best to stand them in a block of polystyrene or place in tall glasses. It's essential that the cookies are small enough to fit inside the plastic tube so you may need to trim them down slightly. Don't be afraid to push the layers of filling together but do it slowly and firmly. Once filled and topped with the lids they can be chilled on their sides in the refrigerator, but you may want to top up the fillings before serving.

Dyeing cake batter – to get a good depth of colour in a cake batter you'll need to add a fair bit of colouring, but add it gradually and mix well after each addition. Paste or gels give the best colour and won't affect the consistency of the batter but if you only have liquid colouring then add another spoonful of flour to the batter to compensate for the extra moisture.

Deep-frying – use a light, flavourless oil to deep-fry and, for the best results, a sugar thermometer to make sure the oil is the correct temperature. Only fry a few doughnuts at a time otherwise the temperature of the oil will drop and the doughnuts will end up soggy and greasy. Turn the doughnuts 2–3 times during frying to ensure even colouring and drain thoroughly, then place on scrunched greaseproof paper or kitchen paper to allow any excess oil to drain off.

COOKIES & CAKES

RED VELVET CRINKLE COOKIES

MAKES: 22
PREP: 25 MINS, PLUS COOLING
COOK: 14–16 MINS

BASED ON THE CLASSIC RED VELVET CAKE, THESE COOKIES HAVE THE SAME DEEP RED COLOUR AND RICH CHOCOLATE FLAVOUR BUT WITH A CRISP AND CRUNCHY TEXTURE!

- 115 G/4 OZ BUTTER, SOFTENED
- 200 G/7 OZ LIGHT MUSCOVADO SUGAR
- 2 EGGS, BEATEN
- 2 TSP RED LIQUID FOOD COLOURING
- 280 G/10 OZ PLAIN FLOUR
- 1 TSP BAKING POWDER
- ¼ TSP BICARBONATE OF SODA
- 40 G/1½ OZ COCOA POWDER
- 25 G/1 OZ ICING SUGAR

1 Put the butter and sugar into a large bowl and beat with a hand-held electric mixer until pale and fluffy. Gradually beat in the eggs, then beat in the food colouring.

2 Sift together the flour, baking powder, bicarbonate of soda and cocoa powder into the mixture. Stir with a wooden spoon to make a soft dough. Cover and chill in the refrigerator for 30–40 minutes, or until the dough is firm enough to shape.

3 Preheat the oven to 190°C/375°F/Gas Mark 5. Line two large baking sheets with baking paper.

4 Divide the dough into 22 pieces, then shape each piece into a ball. Sift the icing sugar onto a plate. Roll each ball of dough in the sugar to coat it completely, then place the balls on the baking sheets. Flatten each ball with your fingertips to a 6-cm/2½-inch round.

5 Bake in the preheated oven for 14–16 minutes, or until just set. Leave to cool on the baking sheets for 5 minutes, then transfer to a wire rack to cool completely. Sprinkle any remaining icing sugar over the cookies before serving.

Cook's Tip

THESE COOKIES ARE BEST EATEN
ON THE DAY OF MAKING, ALTHOUGH
THEY WILL KEEP IN AN AIRTIGHT
CONTAINER FOR 2–3 DAYS.

MAPLE BACON CUPCAKES

MAKES: 12
PREP: 30 MINS
COOK: 45–50 MINS

BASED ON THE POPULAR AMERICAN BREAKFAST DISH OF PANCAKES WITH MAPLE SYRUP AND BACON, THIS QUIRKY TWIST ON A CLASSIC COMBINATION PROVES THAT EVERYTHING IS BETTER WITH BACON – EVEN CUPCAKES.

For the candied bacon

- 8 BACON RASHERS
- 55 G/2 OZ SOFT LIGHT BROWN SUGAR

For the cupcakes

- 190 G/6¾ OZ PLAIN FLOUR
- 1½ TSP BAKING POWDER
- ¼ TSP SALT
- 115 G/4 OZ UNSALTED BUTTER, AT ROOM TEMPERATURE
- 100 G/3½ OZ CASTER SUGAR
- 125 ML/4 FL OZ MAPLE SYRUP
- 1 TSP VANILLA EXTRACT
- 2 LARGE EGGS
- 125 ML/4 FL OZ MILK

For the frosting

- 4 EGG WHITES
- 200 G/7 OZ SUGAR
- ¼ TSP CREAM OF TARTAR
- 2 TBSP MAPLE SYRUP
- 2 TSP MAPLE EXTRACT

1 Preheat the oven to 180°C/350°F/Gas Mark 4 and line a 12-hole cupcake tin with paper cases.

2 To make the candied bacon, line a baking sheet with foil. Cut four of the rashers into three lengths each (the other four rashers can be left whole). Place on the prepared sheet and sprinkle half the sugar over. Turn the bacon over and repeat with the remaining sugar. Bake in the preheated oven for 25–30 minutes, until it is brown and crisp. Remove from the oven (leave the oven on) and allow to cool on kitchen paper. Crumble the whole rashers of bacon, reserving the individual lengths for decoration.

3 To make the cupcakes, combine the flour, baking powder and salt in a medium-sized bowl. Put the butter and sugar into another large bowl and beat with an electric hand-held mixer until pale yellow and fluffy. Add the maple syrup and beat until combined. Add the vanilla extract, then add the eggs, one at a time, beating after each addition, until combined. Add half the flour mixture and beat until incorporated. Add the milk and beat until incorporated. Add the remaining flour mixture and mix until just incorporated. Stir in the crumbled candied bacon.

4 Scoop the batter into the paper cases, then bake in the oven for about 20 minutes. Leave to cool in the tin for 1–2 minutes, then transfer to a wire rack to cool completely.

5 To make the frosting, heat some water in the base of a double boiler until it is just simmering. Put the egg whites, sugar and cream of tartar into the top of the double boiler and mix to combine. Set over the simmering water (the pan should be touching the water) and whisk constantly for about 5 minutes, until the sugar is completely dissolved and the mixture is warm. Remove from the heat and, using an electric mixer fitted with a whisk attachment, beat the mixture on high speed for about 7 minutes, until it holds stiff, glossy peaks. Add the maple syrup and the maple extract and beat until combined. Scoop the frosting into a piping bag fitted with your favourite tip.

6 When the cupcakes are completely cool, pipe the frosting onto them. Decorate each cupcake with pieces of candied bacon.

VIENNESE FINGERS

MAKES: 16
PREP: 20 MINS
COOK: 10–15 MINS

DON'T WORRY IF YOU'RE NOT AN EXPERT AT PIPING, THESE CRUMBLY, DELICATE BISCUITS WILL STILL LOOK GREAT ONCE BAKED AND DIPPED IN DELICIOUS PLAIN CHOCOLATE.

- 100 G/3½ OZ UNSALTED BUTTER, PLUS EXTRA FOR GREASING
- 25 G/1 OZ GOLDEN CASTER SUGAR
- ½ TSP VANILLA EXTRACT
- 100 G/3½ OZ SELF-RAISING FLOUR
- 100 G/3½ OZ PLAIN CHOCOLATE

1 Preheat the oven to 160°C/325°F/Gas Mark 3. Lightly grease two baking sheets.

2 Place the butter, sugar and vanilla extract in a bowl and cream together until pale and fluffy. Stir in the flour, mixing evenly to a fairly stiff dough.

3 Place the mixture in a piping bag fitted with a large star nozzle and pipe about 16 fingers, each 6 cm/2½ inches long, onto the prepared baking sheets spaced well apart.

4 Bake in the preheated oven for 10–15 minutes, until golden brown. Leave to cool on the baking sheets for a few minutes, then transfer the biscuits to wire racks to cool completely.

5 Break the chocolate into a small heatproof bowl set over a saucepan of gently simmering water until melted. Remove from the heat. Dip one end of each biscuit into the chocolate to coat, then place on a sheet of baking paper and leave to set.

Cook's Tip

THESE LIGHT AND BUTTERY BISCUITS ARE BEST EATEN SOON AFTER BAKING WITH A CUP OF COFFEE.

MINI OMBRE CAKES

MAKES: 6
PREP: 45 MINS
COOK: 18–20 MINS

DELICATELY SHADED ROUNDS OF SPONGE SANDWICHED TOGETHER WITH A SWEET AND CREAMY PINK FROSTING, THESE DIVINE MINIATURE CAKES WILL BE THE STAR ATTRACTIONS FOR THAT SPECIAL AFTERNOON TEA.

- 225 G/8 OZ SELF-RAISING FLOUR
- 225 G/8 OZ BUTTER, SOFTENED, PLUS EXTRA FOR GREASING
- 225 G/8 OZ CASTER SUGAR
- 4 LARGE EGGS
- 1 TSP VANILLA EXTRACT
- 1 TBSP MILK
- PINK FOOD COLOURING PASTE

For the frosting

- 175 G/6 OZ UNSALTED BUTTER, SOFTENED
- 6 TBSP DOUBLE CREAM
- 350 G/12 OZ ICING SUGAR
- PINK FOOD COLOURING PASTE
- SHIMMER HUNDREDS AND THOUSANDS, TO DECORATE

1 Preheat the oven to 180°C/350°F/Gas Mark 4. Grease four 20-cm/8-inch round sandwich cake tins and line the bases with baking paper.

2 Sift the flour into a large mixing bowl and add the butter, sugar, eggs, vanilla extract and milk. Using a hand-held electric mixer, beat for 1–2 minutes until pale and creamy. Divide the mixture evenly between four bowls.

3 Beat the food colouring paste into three of the bowls of mixture to give three distinctly different shades of colour, from pale pink to very deep pink. Leave the fourth bowl of mixture plain. Spoon each bowl of mixture into a prepared tin and gently level the surface.

4 Bake in the preheated oven for 18–20 minutes, or until risen and just firm to the touch. Leave to cool in the tins for 5 minutes, then turn out onto wire racks to cool completely.

5 To make the frosting, put the butter into a bowl and beat with a hand-held electric mixer for 1–2 minutes until pale and creamy. Beat in the cream, then gradually sift in the sugar and continue beating for 2–3 minutes until the frosting is light and fluffy. Beat in a little pink food colouring.

6 To assemble the cakes, use a 6-cm/2½-inch round cutter to stamp six rounds from each sponge. Sandwich four of the different coloured sponge rounds together in a stack with some of the frosting. Start with the darkest sponge at the base and finish with the lightest at the top. Repeat with the remaining rounds and frosting to make six cakes in total.

7 Spoon the remaining frosting into a piping bag fitted with a large star-shaped nozzle. Pipe a rosette on the top of each cake and decorate with shimmer hundreds and thousands.

Cook's Tip

TO MAKE MINI RAINBOW CAKES INSTEAD, COLOUR THE SPONGES RED, ORANGE, GREEN AND BLUE, AND SANDWICH TOGETHER WITH PALE YELLOW FROSTING.

CHOC CHIP COOKIE SUNDAE PUSH POPS

MAKES: 10
PREP: 40 MINS, PLUS COOLING AND CHILLING
COOK: 12–14 MINS

ENJOY A SCRUMPTIOUS LAYERED COOKIE, CREAM AND CHOCOLATE CREATION WITH THESE FUN PUSH POPS. THE SIMPLE PLASTIC CONTAINERS ARE AVAILABLE TO BUY ONLINE AND THEY'RE RE-USABLE TOO!

For the cookies
- 85 G/3 OZ BUTTER, SOFTENED, PLUS EXTRA FOR GREASING
- 70 G/2½ OZ CASTER SUGAR
- 1 EGG YOLK
- 115 G/4 OZ PLAIN FLOUR, PLUS EXTRA FOR DUSTING
- 1 TBSP COCOA POWDER
- 2 TBSP CHOCOLATE CHIPS

For the fudge sauce
- 85 G/3 OZ PLAIN CHOCOLATE, BROKEN INTO PIECES
- 25 G/1 OZ BUTTER
- 1 TBSP GOLDEN SYRUP

To assemble
- 400 ML/14 FL OZ DOUBLE CREAM
- 1 TBSP CHOCOLATE SUGAR STRANDS
- 10 FRESH CHERRIES, STALKS ON

You will also need
- 10 PLASTIC PUSH POP CONTAINERS

1 To make the cookies, put the butter and sugar into a large bowl and beat together until pale and creamy. Beat in the egg yolk, then sift in the flour and cocoa powder and mix to a rough dough. Gather together with your hands and knead lightly on a floured surface until smooth.

2 Divide the dough into two pieces and roll each piece into a 14–cm/5½-inch long log shape. Wrap each log in clingfilm and chill in the refrigerator for 45 minutes.

3 Preheat the oven to 180°C/350°F/Gas Mark 4. Lightly grease two baking sheets. Slice each log of cookie dough into 20 rounds and place on the prepared baking sheets (see Cook's Tip). Top each cookie with 2–3 chocolate chips. Bake in the preheated oven for 12–14 minutes until just firm at the edges. Leave to cool on the baking sheets for 1–2 minutes, then transfer to a wire rack to cool completely.

4 To make the fudge sauce, put the chocolate, butter and golden syrup into a heatproof bowl set over a saucepan of gently simmering water and heat until the chocolate and butter have melted. Remove from the heat and stir until smooth. Leave to cool and thicken for 30 minutes, stirring occasionally.

5 To assemble the push pops, whip the cream in a bowl until it holds stiff peaks, then spoon into a large piping bag fitted with a large star nozzle. Place a cookie in the base of each push pop container. Top with a swirl of cream and a drizzle of fudge sauce. Repeat to make three more layers, finishing with a larger swirl of cream. Sprinkle with the chocolate sugar strands.

6 Repeat with the remaining cookies, cream and sauce to make 10 push pops in total. Top each push pop with a cherry and serve immediately.

Cook's Tip

MAKE SURE THE COOKIE ROUNDS ARE SMALL ENOUGH TO FIT INTO THE PUSH POP CONTAINERS. IF THEY ARE TOO BIG, TRIM THEM BEFORE BAKING USING A 3-CM/1¼-INCH ROUND CUTTER.

PIÑATA PARTY CAKE

SERVES: 10–12
PREP: 1 HR 15 MINS, PLUS COOLING AND CHILLING
COOK: 1 HR 30 MINS

- 450 G/1 LB BUTTER, SOFTENED, PLUS EXTRA FOR GREASING
- 450 G/1 LB CASTER SUGAR
- 8 LARGE EGGS, BEATEN
- 450 G/1 LB SELF-RAISING FLOUR
- 115 G/4 OZ PLAIN FLOUR
- 4 TBSP MILK
- 280 G/10 OZ MIXED SWEETS SUCH AS JELLY BABIES, JELLY BEANS AND SUGAR-COATED CHOCOLATE DROPS
- 2 TBSP PASTEL-COLOURED CONFETTI SUGAR SPRINKLES

For the frosting
- 100 G/3½ OZ WHITE CHOCOLATE, BROKEN INTO PIECES
- 200 G/7 OZ UNSALTED BUTTER, SOFTENED
- 400 G/14 OZ ICING SUGAR, SIFTED

Cook's Tip
FOR A MORE COLOURFUL FROSTING, BEAT IN A LITTLE PINK OR YELLOW FOOD COLOURING PASTE WITH THE MELTED WHITE CHOCOLATE.

CHILDREN WILL LOVE THE SWEETIE SURPRISE HIDDEN INSIDE THIS STUNNING CAKE AND ADULTS WILL MARVEL AT HOW IT WAS MADE! MAKE BOTH CAKES A DAY IN ADVANCE SO THAT THEY CAN FIRM UP BEFORE YOU SCOOP OUT THE CENTRES.

1 Preheat the oven to 160°C/325°F/Gas Mark 3. Thoroughly grease two 2-litre/3½-pint ovenproof bowls.

2 Put the butter and sugar into a large bowl and beat with a hand-held electric mixer until pale and creamy. Gradually beat in the eggs a little at a time. Sift together the self-raising flour and plain flour, then fold into the creamed mixture with the milk.

3 Divide the mixture evenly between the prepared bowls, making a dip in the centre with the back of a spoon. Bake in the preheated oven for 50 minutes, then loosely cover each bowl with foil and bake for a further 20–30 minutes, or until firm to the touch and a skewer inserted into the centre of the cakes comes out clean. Leave to cool in the bowls for 10 minutes, then turn out onto a wire rack to cool completely. Wrap the cold cakes in foil and chill in the refrigerator for 4–5 hours or overnight.

4 To make the frosting, put the chocolate in a heatproof bowl set over a saucepan of gently simmering water and heat until melted. Remove from the heat and leave to cool for 15 minutes. Put the butter into a large bowl and gradually beat in the sugar, then beat in the melted chocolate.

5 To assemble, level the top of each cake with a serrated knife. Scoop out the centres of the cakes, leaving a 4-cm/1½-inch border. Place one cake, cut-side up, on a flat plate or board covered with a sheet of baking paper. Spread some of the frosting around the rim of the cake and pile the sweets and half the coloured sugar sprinkles into the centre. Invert the second cake on top to enclose the sweets and make a globe-shaped cake, pressing down gently to seal.

6 Using a palette knife, spread a thin layer of frosting all over the cake to secure any loose crumbs, then chill in the refrigerator for 1 hour.

7 Spread the remaining frosting in a thick layer over the cake and decorate with the remaining sugar sprinkles. Carefully transfer to a serving plate.

BLACK AND WHITE COOKIES

MAKES: 20
PREP: 15 MINS
COOK: 15 MINS

POPULAR IN AMERICA, THESE SOFT COOKIES – ALSO KNOWN AS 'HALF MOONS' – ARE DECORATED WITH VANILLA AND CHOCOLATE FONDANT.

- 115 G/4 OZ UNSALTED BUTTER, PLUS EXTRA FOR GREASING
- 1 TSP VANILLA EXTRACT
- 175 G/6 OZ CASTER SUGAR
- 2 EGGS, BEATEN
- 300 G/10½ OZ PLAIN FLOUR
- ½ TSP BAKING POWDER
- 200 ML/7 FL OZ MILK

For the fondant icing
- 225 G/8 OZ ICING SUGAR
- 125 ML/4 FL OZ DOUBLE CREAM
- ⅛ TSP VANILLA EXTRACT
- 75 G/2¾ OZ PLAIN CHOCOLATE, BROKEN INTO PIECES

1 Preheat the oven to 190°C/375°F/Gas Mark 5. Grease three baking sheets. Place the butter, vanilla extract and caster sugar in a large bowl. Beat the mixture with a whisk until light and fluffy and then beat in the eggs one at a time.

2 Sift together the flour and baking powder and fold into the creamed mixture, loosening with milk as you go until both are used up and the mixture is of dropping consistency.

3 Drop heaped tablespoonfuls of the mixture, spaced well apart, on the prepared baking sheets. Place in the preheated oven and bake for 15 minutes until turning golden at the edges and light to the touch. Transfer to wire racks to cool completely.

4 To make the fondant icing, sift the icing sugar into a bowl and mix in half the cream and the vanilla extract. The consistency should be thick but spreadable. Using a palette knife, spread half of each cookie with white icing. Now, melt the chocolate in a heatproof bowl set over a saucepan of gently simmering water. Remove from the heat and stir in the remaining cream. Spread the dark icing over the uncoated cookie halves. Leave to set before serving.

Cook's Tip

TO GIVE THESE COOKIES A FRUITY KICK, ADD THE GRATED ZEST OF HALF A SMALL ORANGE TO THE PLAIN CHOCOLATE FONDANT.

RAINBOW CUPCAKES

MAKES: 12
PREP: 45 MINS
COOK: 20 MINS

THESE CUPCAKES, TOPPED WITH WHITE VANILLA BUTTERCREAM, LOOK LIKE ANY OTHER CAKE UNTIL YOU SLICE THEM OPEN TO REVEAL THE COLOURFUL LAYERS WITHIN – PERFECT FOR A CHILDREN'S BIRTHDAY PARTY!

For the cupcakes

- 190 G/6¾ OZ PLAIN FLOUR
- 1½ TSP BAKING POWDER
- ¼ TSP SALT
- 115 G/4 OZ UNSALTED BUTTER, AT ROOM TEMPERATURE
- 4 TBSP VEGETABLE SHORTENING
- 200 G/7 OZ CASTER SUGAR
- 2 TSP VANILLA EXTRACT
- 4 LARGE EGG WHITES
- 125 ML/4 FL OZ MILK
- RED, BLUE, YELLOW AND GREEN FOOD COLOURING GEL
- MULTI-COLOURED HUNDREDS AND THOUSANDS, TO DECORATE

For the frosting

- 3 EGG WHITES
- 150 G/5½ OZ SUGAR
- 115 G/4 OZ UNSALTED BUTTER, AT ROOM TEMPERATURE
- 1 TBSP VANILLA EXTRACT

1 Preheat the oven to 180°C/350°F/Gas Mark 4 and line a 12-hole cupcake tin with paper cases.

2 To make the cupcakes, combine the flour, baking powder and salt in a medium-sized bowl. Put the butter, shortening and sugar into a large bowl and beat with an electric mixer until light and fluffy. Add the vanilla extract, then add the egg whites, one at a time, beating after each addition. Add the milk and half the flour mixture and beat until incorporated. Add the remaining flour mixture and mix.

3 Separate the batter into six small bowls. Colour one bowl of batter red using 8–10 drops of red food colouring. Colour one bowl orange with 8 drops of yellow colouring and 4 drops of red colouring. Colour one bowl yellow with 8 drops of yellow colouring. Colour one bowl green with 8 drops of green colouring. Colour one bowl blue with 8 drops of blue colouring. Colour one bowl purple with 8 drops of red colouring and 4 drops of blue colouring.

4 Scoop the batter into the paper cases one colour at a time, starting with purple. Then drop in a generous spoonful of blue batter. Continue with the green, yellow, orange and red batters. Bake in the preheated oven for about 20 minutes. Leave to cool in the tin for 1–2 minutes, then transfer to a wire rack to cool completely.

5 To make the frosting, heat some water in the base of a double boiler until it is just simmering. Put the egg whites and sugar into the top of the double boiler and mix to combine. Set over the simmering water and whisk constantly for about 5 minutes, until the sugar is completely dissolved. Remove from the heat and, using an electric mixer fitted with a whisk attachment, beat the mixture on high speed for about 5 minutes, until it holds stiff, glossy peaks. Add the butter, a couple of tablespoons at a time, and beat until the mixture holds stiff, fluffy peaks. Finally, add the vanilla extract and beat until just combined. Scoop the frosting into a piping bag fitted with your favourite tip.

6 Pipe the frosting onto the cupcakes, sprinkle over the hundreds and thousands and serve.

Cook's Tip

TO MAKE OMBRE CUPCAKES, COLOUR FOUR BOWLS OF BATTER; THREE WITH GRADUATING SHADES OF THE SAME COLOUR AND THE FOURTH BOWL PLAIN.

2

DOUGHNUTS & PASTRY

PAIN AU CHOCOLAT CINNAMON ROLLS

MAKES: 12
PREP: 20 MINS, PLUS COOLING AND CHILLING
COOK: 15–20 MINS

- 100 G/3½ OZ PLAIN CHOCOLATE, BROKEN INTO PIECES
- 320 G/11 OZ READY-ROLLED PUFF PASTRY
- 25 G/1 OZ UNSALTED BUTTER, MELTED
- 2 TBSP CASTER SUGAR
- 1½ TSP GROUND CINNAMON
- ICING SUGAR, FOR DUSTING (OPTIONAL)

CAN'T DECIDE BETWEEN A SWEET CINNAMON ROLL OR A CRISP AND FLAKY PAIN AU CHOCOLAT? WELL, NOW YOU CAN ENJOY THE BEST OF BOTH WITH THIS DELICIOUS QUICK-AND-EASY HYBRID OF THE TWO!

1 Put the chocolate into a heatproof bowl set over a saucepan of gently simmering water and heat until melted. Remove from the heat, stir until smooth, then leave to cool for 15 minutes, stirring occasionally.

2 Unroll the sheet of puff pastry and place on a board. Generously brush with some of the melted butter. Leave to stand for 10 minutes, then spread the cooled chocolate all over the buttered pastry. Mix together the sugar and cinnamon in a bowl, then sprinkle over the chocolate.

3 Roll up the pastry, Swiss roll-style, from one long side then brush all over with more of the melted butter. Chill in the refrigerator for 15 minutes. Preheat the oven to 220°C/425°F/Gas Mark 7. Use the remaining melted butter to grease a 12-hole cupcake tin.

4 Using a serrated knife, slice the pastry roll into 12 even-sized rounds. Place each round, cut-side up, in a hole in the prepared cupcake tin.

5 Bake in the preheated oven for 15–20 minutes, or until risen and golden brown. Leave to cool in the tin for 5 minutes, then transfer to a wire rack. Dust with icing sugar, if using, and serve warm or cold.

Cook's Tip

FOR A MOCHA-FLAVOURED FILLING, REPLACE THE CINNAMON WITH 2 TEASPOONS FINELY GROUND COFFEE GRANULES.

RASPBERRY AND ROSEWATER ÉCLAIRS

MAKES: 12
PREP: 45 MINS, PLUS COOLING
COOK: 25 MINS

For the choux pastry
- 50 G/1¾ OZ BUTTER
- 150 ML/5 FL OZ WATER
- 70 G/2½ OZ PLAIN FLOUR, SIFTED
- PINCH OF SALT
- 2 EGGS, BEATEN

For the filling
- 300 ML/10 FL OZ DOUBLE CREAM
- 1 TSP ROSEWATER

For the icing
- 200 G/7 OZ ICING SUGAR
- ½ TSP ROSEWATER
- 1½–2 TBSP LUKEWARM WATER
- FEW DROPS PINK LIQUID FOOD COLOURING
- 200 G/7 OZ SMALL RASPBERRIES

THESE CRISP CHOUX PASTRY ÉCLAIRS HAVE A DELICATELY FLAVOURED ROSEWATER CREAM FILLING AND STUNNING FEATHERED ICING DECORATION. SERVE AS A DESSERT WITH A FEW EXTRA RASPBERRIES OR AS PART OF A SUMMER TEA PARTY SPREAD.

1 Preheat the oven to 220°C/425°F/Gas Mark 7. Line a large baking sheet with baking paper.

2 To make the pastry, put the butter and water into a saucepan and heat gently until the butter has melted. Bring to a rolling boil, remove from the heat and quickly beat in the flour and salt until the mixture forms a ball that leaves the sides of the pan clean. Transfer to a bowl and leave to cool for 5 minutes.

3 Gradually beat in the eggs to form a smooth glossy mixture with a soft dropping consistency. Spoon into a piping bag fitted with a 1.5-cm/⅝-inch plain nozzle and pipe twelve 12-cm/4½-inch éclairs onto the prepared baking sheet. Sprinkle a little water around the éclairs.

4 Bake in the preheated oven for 20 minutes, or until golden. Remove from the oven and use the tip of a knife to pierce a hole in each éclair. Return to the oven for a further 5 minutes. Transfer to a wire rack to cool completely.

5 To make the filling, put the cream into a bowl with the rosewater and whip until it holds soft peaks. To make the icing, sift the sugar into another bowl and stir in the rosewater with enough of the water to make a thick, spreadable icing. Remove 2 tablespoons of the icing and add enough food colouring to tint it a deep pink. Spoon it into a paper piping bag and snip off the end.

6 To assemble, split the éclairs lengthways and fill with small spoonfuls of the filling and the raspberries. Gently spread the white icing over the tops of the éclairs.

7 Pipe three thin lines of pink icing along the length of each éclair, then drag the tip of a cocktail stick backwards and forwards through the icing to create a feathered effect. Leave to set before serving.

Cook's Tip

FILL AND ICE 2–3 ÉCLAIRS AT A TIME, OTHERWISE THE ICING WILL SET BEFORE YOU HAVE A CHANCE TO CREATE THE FEATHERED EFFECT.

S'MORES DOUGHNUTS

MAKES: 12
PREP: 45 MINS, PLUS PROVING
COOK: 16 MINS

A QUIRKY TAKE ON THE POPULAR S'MORES COOKIES, THESE DECADENT DOUGHNUTS ARE BRIMMING WITH A DELICIOUS MOLTEN CHOCOLATE AND MARSHMALLOW FILLING.

- 150 ML/5 FL OZ MILK
- 25 G/1 OZ WHITE VEGETABLE FAT
- 300 G/10½ OZ STRONG WHITE FLOUR, PLUS EXTRA FOR DUSTING AND KNEADING
- ¼ TSP SALT
- 1½ TSP EASY-BLEND DRIED YEAST
- 2 TBSP CASTER SUGAR, PLUS EXTRA FOR COATING
- 1 LARGE EGG, BEATEN
- 12 SMALL SQUARES PLAIN CHOCOLATE
- 48 MINI WHITE MARSHMALLOWS
- OIL, FOR DEEP-FRYING AND GREASING
- 1 SMALL DIGESTIVE BISCUIT, CRUSHED

For the glaze
- 55 G/2 OZ ICING SUGAR, SIFTED
- 2 TBSP WATER

1 Put the milk and vegetable fat into a small saucepan over a low heat and heat until the fat has melted. Leave to cool for 5 minutes.

2 Sift the flour into a large bowl and stir in the salt, yeast and sugar. Pour in the milk mixture and the egg, and mix to a soft dough. Turn out the dough onto a floured surface and knead for 5–6 minutes, until smooth and elastic, adding a little more flour if needed.

3 Place the dough in a clean bowl, cover and leave in a warm place for 1 hour, or until doubled in size. Line a large baking sheet with baking paper.

4 Knock back the dough and divide into 12 even pieces. Roll out each piece to a 9-cm/3½-inch round and place a square of chocolate and four mini marshmallows in the centre. Gather up the dough to enclose the filling, tightly pinching the edges together to seal. Place on the prepared baking sheet, join-side down, and flatten each doughnut slightly with the palm of your hand. Cover with lightly oiled clingfilm and leave to stand in a warm place for 8–10 minutes, until puffy.

5 In a large saucepan or deep-fryer heat enough oil for deep-frying to 180–190°C/350–375°F, or until a cube of bread browns in 30 seconds. Fry the doughnuts, three at a time, for 1–2 minutes on each side or until golden. Remove and drain on kitchen paper.

6 To make the glaze, put the icing sugar and water into a bowl and beat together until smooth. Dip the top of each warm doughnut in the glaze and sprinkle over the biscuit crumbs. Serve warm.

Cook's Tip

DON'T TRY TO FRY MORE THAN THREE AT A TIME AS THIS MAY CAUSE THE TEMPERATURE OF THE OIL TO DROP AND MAKE YOUR DOUGHNUTS SOGGY.

COCONUT BROWNIE PIE POPS

MAKES: 14
PREP: 20 MINS, PLUS COOLING
COOK: 16–18 MINS

MOVE OVER CAKE POPS, HERE COME THE PIE POPS – DELICIOUS INDIVIDUAL PIES BAKED ON THEIR OWN LOLLIPOP STICKS. THEY CAN BE MADE IN ADVANCE AND ARE PERFECT FOR KIDS' PARTIES OR PICNICS.

- 55 G/2 OZ PLAIN CHOCOLATE, BROKEN INTO PIECES
- 25 G/1 OZ BUTTER, PLUS EXTRA FOR GREASING
- 1 EGG, BEATEN
- 40 G/1½ OZ LIGHT MUSCOVADO SUGAR
- 70 G/2½ OZ PLAIN FLOUR, PLUS EXTRA FOR DUSTING
- 25 G/1 OZ DESICCATED COCONUT
- 500 G/1 LB 2 OZ READY-MADE SHORTCRUST PASTRY
- 2 TSP COLD WATER

To assemble
- 14 LOLLIPOP STICKS

1 Put the chocolate and butter into a heatproof bowl set over a saucepan of gently simmering water and heat until melted. Remove from the heat, stir until smooth, then leave to cool for 10 minutes, stirring occasionally.

2 Put the beaten egg into a bowl, reserving 1 tablespoon for glazing the pies. Add the sugar, then beat together until combined. Beat in the chocolate mixture. Sift in the flour and fold in with the coconut. The mixture should be quite stiff.

3 Preheat the oven to 190°C/375°F/Gas Mark 5. Grease two large baking sheets. Roll out half the pastry on a lightly floured work surface to a thickness of 3 mm/⅛ inch. Using a 7-cm/2¾-inch round cutter, stamp out 14 rounds and transfer to the prepared baking sheets.

4 Put a heaped teaspoon of the chocolate brownie mixture in the centre of each round and flatten slightly. Push a lollipop stick into the brownie filling. Roll out the remaining pastry and stamp out a further 14 rounds.

5 Lightly brush the pastry edges around the filling with a little water then top with the rounds, pressing together firmly. Crimp and seal the edges of each pie with the tines of a fork.

6 Mix the cold water into the reserved beaten egg and brush over the pies. Bake in the preheated oven for 16–18 minutes, or until the pastry is pale golden. Leave to cool on the baking sheets for 5 minutes, then carefully transfer to a wire rack to cool completely (the sticks will be hot).

Cook's Tip
FOR A FRUITY FILLING, REPLACE THE BROWNIE MIXTURE WITH 1 TABLESPOON OF CANNED FRUIT PIE FILLING OR FINELY CHOPPED FRESH FRUIT, SUCH AS APPLE OR PEACH.

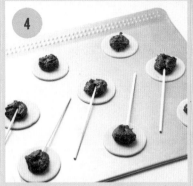

SALTED CARAMEL MINI ÉCLAIRS

MAKES: 15
PREP: 40 MINS, PLUS COOLING
COOK: 20 MINS

TREAT YOUR TASTEBUDS WITH THESE BITE-SIZED SENSATIONS. THEY'RE A HEAVENLY COMBINATION OF CRISP CHOUX PASTRY, COFFEE CREAM FILLING AND A SWEET AND SALTY BUTTER CARAMEL GLAZE.

For the choux pastry

- 50 G/1¾ OZ BUTTER
- 150 ML/5 FL OZ WATER
- 70 G/2½ OZ PLAIN FLOUR, SIFTED
- PINCH OF SALT
- 2 EGGS, BEATEN

For the caramel glaze

- 150 G/5½ OZ GRANULATED SUGAR
- 3 TBSP COLD WATER
- 70 G/2½ OZ LIGHTLY SALTED BUTTER
- PINCH OF SEA SALT
- 4 TBSP DOUBLE CREAM

To assemble

- 300 ML/10 FL OZ DOUBLE CREAM
- 2 TSP COFFEE AND CHICORY EXTRACT
- 1 SHEET EDIBLE GOLD LEAF OR 1 TBSP GOLD HUNDREDS AND THOUSANDS

1 Preheat the oven to 220°C/425°F/Gas Mark 7. Line two large baking sheets with baking paper.

2 To make the pastry, put the butter and water into a saucepan and heat gently until the butter has melted. Bring to a rolling boil, remove from the heat and quickly beat in the flour and salt until the mixture forms a ball that leaves the sides of the pan clean. Transfer to a bowl and leave to cool for 5 minutes.

3 Gradually beat in the eggs to form a smooth, glossy mixture with a soft dropping consistency. Spoon into a piping bag fitted with a 1-cm/½-inch plain nozzle and pipe fifteen 7-cm/2¾-inch mini éclairs onto the prepared baking sheets. Sprinkle a little water around the éclairs.

4 Bake in the preheated oven for 15 minutes, or until golden. Remove from the oven and use the tip of a knife to pierce a hole in the end of each éclair. Return to the oven for a further 5 minutes. Transfer to a wire rack and leave to cool completely.

5 To make the glaze, put the sugar and water into a heavy-based saucepan. Heat gently, stirring, until the sugar has dissolved, then bring to the boil and continue boiling, without stirring, until a deep golden caramel forms. Remove from the heat and leave to stand for 2 minutes, then stir in the butter and salt. Use a balloon whisk to whisk in the double cream and continue whisking until you have a smooth caramel sauce. Pour into a heatproof bowl and leave to cool and thicken for about 30 minutes, stirring occasionally.

6 To assemble the éclairs, put the cream into a bowl with the coffee and chicory extract and whip until it holds soft peaks. Spoon into a piping bag fitted with a 5-mm/¼-inch plain nozzle. Use the tip of a knife to make the holes at the end of each éclair a little larger. Pipe the cream into the éclairs through the holes.

7 Gently dip the top of each filled éclair in the caramel and place on a wire rack. Use the tip of a fine paintbrush to dot a few tiny specks of gold leaf onto the caramel. Leave in a cool place to set before serving.

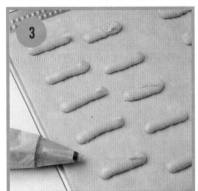

Cook's Tip

SPRINKLING A LITTLE WATER AROUND THE ÉCLAIRS WILL CREATE STEAM IN THE OVEN AND HELP THE CHOUX PASTRY PUFF UP.

FUNFETTI CINNAMON ROLLS

MAKES: 16
PREP: 40 MINS, PLUS PROVING
COOK: 15–20 MINS

WITH THE ADDED BONUS OF A CREAMY SOFT CHEESE FROSTING DECORATED WITH MASSES OF COLOURFUL SUGAR SPRINKLES, THESE CINNAMON ROLLS LOOK AND TASTE FANTASTIC.

- 450 G/1 LB STRONG WHITE FLOUR, PLUS EXTRA FOR DUSTING
- ¼ TSP SALT
- 1½ TSP EASY-BLEND DRIED YEAST
- 40 G/1½ OZ CASTER SUGAR
- 55 G/2 OZ BUTTER, MELTED, PLUS EXTRA FOR GREASING
- 1 EGG, BEATEN
- 200 ML/7 FL OZ LUKEWARM MILK
- VEGETABLE OIL, FOR OILING

For the filling
- 50 G/1¾ OZ BUTTER, SOFTENED
- 50 G/1¾ OZ CASTER SUGAR
- 1 TSP GROUND CINNAMON
- 1 TBSP MULTI-COLOURED NONPAREILS OR HUNDREDS AND THOUSANDS

For the frosting
- 25 G/1 OZ BUTTER, SOFTENED
- 85 G/3 OZ FULL-FAT SOFT CHEESE, AT ROOM TEMPERATURE
- 70 G/2½ OZ ICING SUGAR, SIFTED
- 2 TSP MULTI-COLOURED NONPAREILS OR HUNDREDS AND THOUSANDS

1 Sift together the flour and salt into a large bowl. Stir in the yeast and sugar and make a well in the centre. Beat together the butter, egg and milk in a jug, then pour into the well. Mix to a soft dough, then turn out onto a floured work surface and knead for 5–6 minutes until smooth and elastic, adding a little more flour if the dough is too sticky.

2 Place the dough in a clean bowl, cover with oiled clingfilm and leave in a warm place for about 1¼ hours, or until the dough has doubled in size. Grease a 23-cm/9-inch square shallow cake tin.

3 Turn out the dough onto a floured work surface and lightly knead for 1 minute. Roll out to a 40 x 23-cm/16 x 9-inch rectangle. To make the filling, spread the softened butter over the dough, then sprinkle with the sugar, cinnamon and nonpareils.

4 Preheat the oven to 200°C/400°F/Gas Mark 6. Roll up the dough, Swiss roll-style, from one long side, then use a serrated knife to slice it into 16 rounds. Arrange the rounds, cut-side up, in the prepared tin. Cover loosely with oiled clingfilm and leave to stand in a warm place for about 30 minutes, or until almost doubled in size.

5 Bake in the preheated oven for 15–20 minutes, or until risen and golden. Leave to cool in the tin for 15 minutes, then carefully turn out onto a wire rack to cool a little.

6 To make the frosting, beat together the butter and soft cheese until smooth then beat in the icing sugar. Spread over the warm rolls, then scatter over the nonpareils. Serve warm or cold.

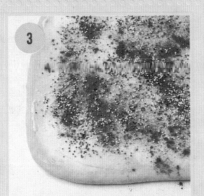

Cook's Tip

THE BEST PLACE TO LEAVE THE DOUGH TO RISE IS CLOSE TO A WARM OVEN AND AWAY FROM ANY COLD DRAUGHTS.

COOKIES AND CREAM DOUGHNUTS

MAKES: 12
PREP: 45 MINS, PLUS RISING
COOK: 20 MINS

THESE DOUGHNUTS MAKE DIVINE USE OF THE EVER-POPULAR FLAVOUR COMBINATION OF COOKIES AND CREAM, AND ARE BEST SERVED WHILE STILL A LITTLE WARM.

- 175 ML/6 FL OZ MILK
- 25 G/1 OZ BUTTER
- 350 G/12 OZ STRONG WHITE FLOUR, PLUS EXTRA FOR DUSTING AND KNEADING
- ¼ TSP SALT
- 1½ TSP EASY-BLEND DRIED YEAST
- 25 G/1 OZ CASTER SUGAR, PLUS EXTRA FOR COATING
- 1 EGG, BEATEN
- OIL, FOR DEEP-FRYING AND GREASING
- 4 TBSP SEEDLESS RASPBERRY JAM

For the filling
- 450 ML/16 FL OZ DOUBLE CREAM
- 70 G/2½ OZ CHOCOLATE SANDWICH COOKIES

For the glaze
- 140 G/5 OZ ICING SUGAR
- 2 TBSP WATER

1 Put the milk and butter into a small saucepan over a low heat and heat until the butter has melted. Leave to cool for 5 minutes.

2 Sift the flour into a large bowl and stir in the salt, yeast and sugar. Pour in the milk mixture and the egg, and mix to a soft dough. Turn out the dough onto a floured surface and knead for 5–6 minutes, until smooth and elastic, adding a little more flour if needed.

3 Put the dough into a bowl, cover and leave in a warm place for 1 hour, or until doubled in size. Line two large baking sheets with baking paper.

4 Knock back the dough and roll out on a lightly floured surface to a thickness of 1 cm/½ inch. Using a 9-cm/3½-inch doughnut cutter, stamp out eight doughnuts. Lightly re-knead the trimmings, roll out and stamp out another four doughnuts. Place on the prepared baking sheets. Cover with lightly oiled clingfilm and leave in a warm place for 10 minutes, until puffy.

5 Heat enough oil for deep-frying in a large saucepan or deep-fryer to 180–190°C/350–375°F, or until a cube of bread browns in 30 seconds. Add the doughnuts, 2–3 at a time, and fry on each side for 1–2 minutes, or until golden. Remove and drain on kitchen paper. Leave to cool.

6 To make the filling, whip the cream until it holds soft peaks. Roughly crush the cookies and fold into the cream, reserving 2 tablespoons of crushed cookies for decoration.

7 To make the glaze, sift the icing sugar into a bowl and beat in the water until smooth.

8 Halve each doughnut horizontally and spread the jam on the bottom halves. Spoon the filling on top of the jam. Dip each top half in the glaze and place on top of the creamy cookie filling. Sprinkle over the reserved crushed cookies and leave to set before serving.

Cook's Tip

WITH A LOVELY SWEET CREAM FILLING, THESE DOUGHNUTS ARE PERFECT FOR A SPECIAL OCCASION. THEY CAN BE MADE THE DAY BEFORE AND KEPT IN THE REFRIGERATOR OVERNIGHT.

LEMON CHURROS WITH ORANGE DIPPING SAUCE

MAKES: 20
PREP: 20 MINS
COOK: 25 MINS

- 100 G/3½ OZ UNSALTED BUTTER, DICED
- 300 ML/10 FL OZ WATER
- 140 G/5 OZ PLAIN FLOUR, SIFTED
- LARGE PINCH OF SALT
- 2 LARGE EGGS, BEATEN
- FINELY GRATED RIND OF 1 LARGE LEMON
- OIL, FOR DEEP-FRYING
- ICING SUGAR, FOR DUSTING

For the orange sauce

- 1 TBSP ARROWROOT
- 300 ML/10 FL OZ FRESH ORANGE JUICE
- 40 G/1½ OZ CASTER SUGAR

SOMETIMES CALLED 'SPANISH DOUGHNUTS', THESE DELECTABLE LITTLE DOUGH PASTRIES ARE TRADITIONALLY SERVED AT BREAKFAST, DUSTED IN SUGAR AND DIPPED IN HOT CHOCOLATE.

1 To make the orange sauce, blend the arrowroot to a smooth paste with 2 tablespoons of the orange juice and set aside. Put the remaining juice and the sugar into a small saucepan over a low heat and heat until the sugar has dissolved. Add the blended arrowroot and simmer gently, stirring constantly, for 4–5 minutes, until just thickened. Remove from the heat, cover and keep warm.

2 Put the butter and water into a large saucepan over a medium heat and heat until the butter has melted. Bring to the boil, remove from the heat and tip in the flour and salt. Quickly beat until the mixture forms a ball that leaves the sides of the pan clean. Leave to cool for 5 minutes, then gradually beat in the eggs to form a smooth, glossy mixture. Beat in the lemon rind.

3 Heat enough oil for deep-frying in a large saucepan or deep-fryer to 180–190°C/350–375°F, or until a cube of bread browns in 30 seconds. Spoon the paste into a large piping bag fitted with a large star nozzle and pipe 4–5 short loops of the mixture into the hot oil. Fry, turning frequently, for 2–3 minutes, until crisp and golden. Remove with a slotted spoon and drain on kitchen paper. Repeat until you have used up all the batter. Thickly dust the hot churros with icing sugar and serve immediately with the orange sauce for dipping.

Cook's Tip

THE TANGY LEMON FLAVOURING
ENSURES THAT THESE WARM
MEXICAN-STYLE DOUGHNUTS
ARE NOT TOO SWEET,
EVEN WITH A GENEROUS
DUSTING OF ICING SUGAR.

3

SWEETS & FANCIES

GRASSHOPPER MINT CHOCOLATE BARK

MAKES: 18–20 PIECES
PREP: 20 MINS, PLUS COOLING AND CHILLING
COOK: 20 MINS

THIS MINT-FLAVOURED CHOCOLATE BARK IS THE SIMPLEST TREAT TO MAKE BUT LOOKS AMAZING AND TASTES WONDERFUL TOO! BREAK IT INTO SHARDS AND SERVE AS AN AFTER-DINNER TREAT WITH BLACK COFFEE.

- VEGETABLE OIL, FOR OILING
- 350 G/12 OZ PLAIN CHOCOLATE, BROKEN INTO PIECES
- 300 G/10½ OZ WHITE CHOCOLATE, BROKEN INTO PIECES
- 1½ TSP PEPPERMINT EXTRACT
- 1 TSP GREEN LIQUID FOOD COLOURING

1 Lightly oil a 33 x 23-cm/13 x 9-inch Swiss roll tin and line the base and sides with baking paper.

2 Put the plain chocolate in a heatproof bowl set over a saucepan of gently simmering water and heat until melted. Remove from the heat and stir until smooth. Set aside 4 tablespoons of the melted chocolate in a small, heatproof bowl.

3 Pour the remaining melted chocolate into the prepared tin and gently level the surface with a palette knife. Firmly tap the tin on a work surface to remove any air bubbles. Leave to stand for 15 minutes, or until the tin is cool, then chill in the refrigerator for 30–40 minutes, or until firmly set.

4 Put the white chocolate into a separate heatproof bowl set over a saucepan of gently simmering water and heat until melted. Remove from the heat, leave to cool for 5–10 minutes, then beat in the peppermint extract and green food colouring. The chocolate will start to thicken, but continue beating for 1–2 minutes until it becomes a smooth and spreadable consistency.

5 Spoon the mint-flavoured chocolate over the set chocolate and spread quickly with a palette knife (don't worry if the plain chocolate underneath melts slightly). If necessary, re-melt the reserved plain chocolate by placing the bowl over a saucepan of gently simmering water. Drizzle it over the mint chocolate layer and lightly drag a fork through the chocolate to create a swirled effect.

6 Chill in the refrigerator for a further 40–50 minutes, or until the bark is firmly set. Remove from the tin, peel off the paper and break into chunks to serve.

Cook's Tip

FOR AN EXTRA MINTY FLAVOUR, ROUGHLY CRUSH 2–3 MINT HUMBUGS AND SCATTER OVER THE TOP OF THE BARK BEFORE IT SETS.

PIÑA COLADA MARSHMALLOWS

MAKES: 35
PREP: 45 MINS, PLUS SETTING
COOK: ABOUT 20 MINS

THE TROPICAL TANG OF PINEAPPLE JUICE IS THE PERFECT PARTNER TO THE COCONUT LIQUEUR IN THESE MARSHMALLOWS – STRICTLY FOR ADULTS!

- SUNFLOWER OIL, FOR GREASING
- 1 TSP CORNFLOUR
- 1 TSP ICING SUGAR
- 100 G/3½ OZ DESICCATED COCONUT
- PINK FOOD COLOURING PASTE

For the marshmallows

- 100 ML/3½ FL OZ PINEAPPLE JUICE
- 100 ML/3½ FL OZ COLD WATER
- 450 G/1 LB GRANULATED SUGAR
- 100 ML/3½ FL OZ HOT WATER
- 25 G/1 OZ GELATINE
- 2 LARGE EGG WHITES
- 2 TBSP COCONUT LIQUEUR OR RUM, WARMED
- YELLOW FOOD COLOURING PASTE

Cook's Tip

TAKE CARE WHEN BOILING THE SUGAR SYRUP AND ADDING IT TO THE EGG WHITES AS IT WILL BE EXTREMELY HOT.

1 Lightly oil a 28 x 18-cm/11 x 7-inch traybake tin. Line the base and two short sides with baking paper, then lightly oil the paper. To make the coating, sift together the cornflour and icing sugar into a bowl. Use a little of this mixture to dust the lined tin.

2 Place the coconut in a bag with a tiny amount of pink food colouring paste. Seal the bag and rub it between your hands until the coconut is evenly coloured pale pink. Sprinkle half the coconut in the base of the tin, reserving the remainder.

3 To make the marshmallow, put the pineapple juice, cold water and granulated sugar in a small, deep saucepan. Heat gently, stirring constantly with a wooden spoon, until the sugar has dissolved. Bring the syrup to the boil and boil, without stirring, for about 5 minutes until the mixture reaches around 120°C/248°F on a sugar thermometer.

4 Meanwhile, put the hot water into a small bowl, sprinkle over the gelatine and stir until dissolved and the liquid is clear. Put the egg whites into the bowl of a free-standing electric mixer and whisk until they hold stiff peaks.

5 When the syrup has reached the correct temperature, remove the pan from the heat and add the gelatine mixture – it will fizz and bubble. Leave to stand for a few seconds, then slowly pour the syrup into a large, heatproof jug.

6 Set the mixer on a low speed and gradually add the hot syrup to the egg whites in a slow stream. When all the syrup has been added, increase the speed to high and whisk for 10 minutes until the mixture leaves a trail on the surface when the whisk is lifted. Whisk in the liqueur and a little food colouring paste to turn the mixture pale yellow.

7 Pour the mixture into the prepared tin and sprinkle over the remaining pink coconut. Leave to set, uncovered, in a cool, dry place for 4–5 hours. Run a knife along the unlined sides of the tin to release the marshmallow. Using the lining paper, gently lift out the marshmallow and place on a chopping board. Cut into 35 squares and serve.

CINNAMON-SUGARED MIXED NUTS

SERVES: 8–10
PREP: 10 MINS
COOK: 35–40 MINS

THESE CRISP SUGARED AND SPICED NUTS ARE GREAT FOR SERVING AS SWEET NIBBLES BUT ALSO MAKE A LOVELY FOODIE GIFT – SIMPLY PACK INTO SMALL PRESERVING JARS AND FINISH WITH RIBBON AND A GIFT TAG.

- 1 EGG WHITE
- 1 TBSP WATER
- 1/2 TSP VANILLA EXTRACT
- 125 G/4 1/2 OZ PECAN NUTS
- 115 G/4 OZ WHOLE UNBLANCHED ALMONDS
- 70 G/2 1/2 OZ CASHEW NUTS
- 55 G/2 OZ GRANULATED SUGAR
- 55 G/2 OZ LIGHT MUSCOVADO SUGAR
- 1 1/2 TSP GROUND CINNAMON
- PINCH OF SALT

1 Preheat the oven to 150°C/300°F/Gas Mark 2. Line a large baking sheet with baking paper.

2 Put the egg white, water and vanilla extract into a bowl and beat with a fork until just frothy.

3 Add the pecan nuts, almonds and cashew nuts and stir to coat thoroughly in the mixture. Mix together the granulated sugar, muscovado sugar, cinnamon and salt, and stir into the nuts. Mix well to completely coat the nuts. Spread the nuts in a single layer on the prepared baking sheet.

4 Bake in the preheated oven for 35–40 minutes, turning 2–3 times with a fork, until all the nuts are crisp and golden. Leave to cool completely on the baking sheet before serving.

Cook's Tip

THIS RECIPE WORKS JUST AS WELL WITH OTHER NUTS, SUCH AS WALNUTS, HAZELNUTS OR MACADAMIA NUTS.

CHOCOLATE MERINGUE KISSES

MAKES: 40
PREP: 40 MINS
COOK: 45 MINS

ELEGANT LITTLE 'KISSES' OF MELT-IN-THE-MOUTH MERINGUE DIPPED IN CHOCOLATE, THESE MAKE A VERY GOOD SWEET CANAPÉ OR GIFT.

- 3 EGG WHITES
- 1 TSP RASPBERRY VINEGAR
- 150 G/5½ OZ CASTER SUGAR
- 1 TSP CORNFLOUR
- 2 TBSP COCOA POWDER, SIFTED
- 200 G/7 OZ PLAIN CHOCOLATE, ROUGHLY CHOPPED

1 Preheat the oven to 160°C/325°F/Gas Mark 3. Line three baking sheets with baking paper.

2 Whisk the egg whites in a large, clean mixing bowl until you have stiff, moist-looking peaks. Gradually whisk in the vinegar and sugar, a tablespoon at a time, until thick and glossy. Using a large metal spoon, gently fold in the cornflour and cocoa powder.

3 Spoon the mixture into a piping bag fitted with a large star nozzle and pipe forty 2.5-cm/1-inch 'kisses' onto the prepared baking sheets.

4 Put the sheets in the preheated oven, then immediately turn the heat down to 120°C/250°F/Gas Mark ½. Bake for 45 minutes, or until crisp on the outside. Transfer the meringues to a wire rack, still on the baking paper, and leave to cool for 1 hour, then gently peel off the paper.

5 Meanwhile, put the chocolate in a heatproof bowl set over a saucepan of gently simmering water and heat until melted. Stir until smooth.

6 Line the baking sheets with more baking paper. Dip the bases of the meringue kisses in the melted chocolate and place them, chocolate-side up, on the prepared baking sheets. Leave to set for 1 hour before serving.

Cook's Tip

DIP THESE LITTLE MERINGUES IN MELTED WHITE CHOCOLATE INSTEAD, OR ADD A LITTLE RED FOOD COLOURING TO MAKE PRETTY PINK KISSES.

CHOCOLATE-DIPPED PUMPKIN SEED BRITTLE

MAKES: 10–12 PIECES
PREP: 10 MINS
COOK: 30 MINS

- 300 G/10½ OZ SUGAR
- 55 G/2 OZ GOLDEN SYRUP
- 100 ML/3½ FL OZ COLD WATER
- 40 G/1½ OZ BUTTER, DICED, PLUS EXTRA FOR GREASING
- ¼ TSP BICARBONATE OF SODA
- 85 G/3 OZ PUMPKIN SEEDS, WARMED
- 50 G/1¾ OZ PLAIN CHOCOLATE, BROKEN INTO PIECES
- ¼ TSP SEA SALT FLAKES (OPTIONAL)

CLASSIC PEANUT BRITTLE IS GIVEN A MAKEOVER WITH CRUNCHY PUMPKIN SEEDS, A LITTLE PLAIN CHOCOLATE AND A SPRINKLING OF SEA SALT. YOU'LL NEED TO USE A SUGAR THERMOMETER AND A HEAVY-BASED SAUCEPAN FOR THE BEST RESULTS.

1 Lightly grease a large, heavy-duty baking sheet. Line a board with baking paper. Put the sugar, golden syrup and water into a large, heavy-based saucepan and heat gently, stirring with a wooden spoon, until the sugar has dissolved. Stir in the butter and heat until melted.

2 Bring the mixture to the boil, without stirring, then cover and boil for 2–3 minutes. Uncover and clip a sugar thermometer to the side of the pan. Continue to boil the mixture steadily, without stirring, until it reaches 154°C/310°F (the 'hard crack' stage) on the thermometer – this will take about 25 minutes (see Cook's Tip).

3 Remove the pan from the heat and stir in the bicarbonate of soda and pumpkin seeds (take care, as the mixture may bubble up). Slowly pour the mixture onto the prepared baking sheet, spreading out to a 30-cm/12-inch square with a palette knife.

4 Leave to stand for a few minutes until the brittle is beginning to set, then mark out about 10 thin strips with a greased long-bladed knife. Leave to stand in a cool place until completely cold and set.

5 Put the chocolate into a small heatproof bowl set over a saucepan of gently simmering water and heat until melted. Remove from the heat and stir until smooth, then leave to cool for 10 minutes.

6 Using a sharp knife, cut through the brittle into long thin strips (some strips may break into shorter pieces). Dip one end of each piece of brittle in the melted chocolate. Place on a wire rack or board and sprinkle the chocolate with a few sea salt flakes, if using. Leave to stand in a cool place until set.

Cook's Tip

DON'T BE TEMPTED TO BOIL
THE MIXTURE TOO RAPIDLY OR IT
MAY BURN AND STICK TO THE
BASE OF THE SAUCEPAN.

CHOCOLATE AND CARAMEL CUPS

MAKES: 12
PREP: 30 MINS, PLUS CHILLING AND COOLING
COOK: 7–8 MINS

- 150 G/5½ OZ PLAIN CHOCOLATE, ROUGHLY CHOPPED
- 115 G/4 OZ GRANULATED SUGAR
- 4 TBSP WATER
- 12 SMALL WALNUT HALVES
- 25 G/1 OZ UNSALTED BUTTER
- 125 ML/4 FL OZ DOUBLE CREAM

IF YOU DON'T HAVE ANY PETIT FOUR CASES, LINE THE SECTIONS OF A MINI MUFFIN TIN WITH SMALL SQUARES OF CLINGFILM, SPREAD MELTED CHOCOLATE OVER THE CLING FILM, THEN PEEL IT AWAY BEFORE SERVING.

1 Line a 12-hole mini muffin tin with paper petit four cases. Line a baking sheet with baking paper.

2 Put the chocolate in a heatproof bowl set over a saucepan of gently simmering water and heat until melted. Put a spoonful of melted chocolate into each paper case, then brush over the sides evenly using a small pastry brush. Chill for 30 minutes in the refrigerator, then brush on a second layer of chocolate, taking care over the sides so there is an even thickness. Cover and chill in the refrigerator.

3 Put the sugar and water into a small heavy-based saucepan. Heat gently for 5 minutes, or until the sugar has dissolved, tilting the pan to mix them together. Increase the heat and boil rapidly without stirring for 4–5 minutes, until the caramel is a deep golden. Remove from the heat, add the walnuts, and stir quickly to coat in the caramel, then lift them out using two forks. Put them on the prepared baking sheet, slightly apart, and reserve the remaining caramel for the filling.

4 Add the butter to the remaining caramel, tilt the pan to mix, then gradually stir in the cream. Transfer to a bowl, leave to cool, then cover and chill in the refrigerator for 1½ hours, or until thick. Lift the chocolate-lined paper cases out of the tin. Spoon the caramel cream into a large piping bag fitted with a large star nozzle and pipe it into the chocolate cups. Chill in the refrigerator until required. Decorate with the caramel walnuts just before serving.

Cook's Tip

OTHER NUTS WOULD WORK WELL IN THIS RECIPE, SUCH AS MACADAMIA NUTS, PECAN NUTS OR HAZELNUTS.

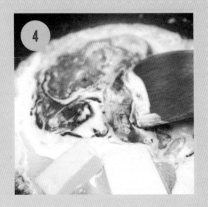

HONEYCOMB SHARDS

MAKES: 20
PREP: 15 MINS
COOK: 10–15 MINS

KNOWN AS HOKEY-POKEY IN AUSTRALIA, THESE LIGHT AND CRUNCHY SHARDS OF HONEYCOMB ARE PERFECT BROKEN INTO BITE-SIZED PIECES OR SIMPLY CRUSHED AND SERVED OVER ICE CREAM.

- A LITTLE SUNFLOWER OIL, FOR OILING
- 175 G/6 OZ CASTER SUGAR
- 100 G/3½ OZ GOLDEN SYRUP
- 100 G/3½ OZ UNSALTED BUTTER, DICED
- 2 TSP BICARBONATE OF SODA

1 Lightly brush a 20-cm/8-inch square baking tin with oil.

2 Put the sugar, syrup and butter into a large heavy-based saucepan. Heat gently until the sugar has dissolved, tilting the pan to mix the ingredients together. Increase the heat and boil rapidly for 4–5 minutes, or until the mixture goes a light golden colour.

3 Add the bicarbonate of soda and stir for a few seconds; be careful as the mixture will expand and bubble.

4 Pour the mixture into the prepared tin. Leave to cool for 5 minutes, or until set. Break the honeycomb into shards and serve.

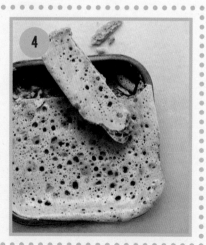

Cook's Tip

TAKE CARE WHEN POURING THE BOILING MIXTURE INTO THE PREPARED TIN AS IT CAN EASILY BUBBLE OVER.

4

SMALL BITES

PEANUT BUTTER AND JAM WHOOPIE PIES

MAKES: 14
PREP: 20 MINS
COOK: 10–12 MINS

BASED ON THE CLASSIC COMBINATION OF PEANUT BUTTER AND JAM, THESE WHOOPIES TAKE 'SANDWICHES' TO ANOTHER LEVEL WITH THEIR SOFT COOKIE HALVES AND FLUFFY PEANUT BUTTERCREAM FILLING.

- 250 G/9 OZ PLAIN FLOUR
- 1 TSP BICARBONATE OF SODA
- LARGE PINCH OF SALT
- 1 TBSP SALTED PEANUTS
- 115 G/4 OZ BUTTER, SOFTENED
- 150 G/5½ OZ LIGHT MUSCOVADO SUGAR
- 1 LARGE EGG, BEATEN
- 150 ML/5 FL OZ BUTTERMILK
- 85 G/3 OZ UNSALTED PEANUTS, FINELY GROUND
- 3 TBSP SEEDLESS RASPBERRY JAM

For the peanut butter buttercream

- 115 G/4 OZ UNSALTED BUTTER, SOFTENED
- 115 G/4 OZ CRUNCHY PEANUT BUTTER
- 140 G/5 OZ ICING SUGAR, SIFTED

1 Preheat the oven to 180°C/350°F/Gas Mark 4. Line 2–3 large baking sheets with baking paper. Sift together the plain flour, bicarbonate of soda and salt in a bowl. Place the salted peanuts in a food processor and whizz them briefly until you have small, roughly chopped pieces. Reserve for assembling the whoopie pies.

2 Place the butter and sugar in a large bowl and beat with a hand-held electric mixer until pale and fluffy. Beat in the egg, followed by half the flour mixture and then the buttermilk. Stir in the rest of the flour mixture and mix until thoroughly incorporated. Fold in the unsalted ground peanuts.

3 Pipe or spoon 28 mounds of the mixture onto the prepared baking sheets. Sprinkle with the chopped salted nuts. Bake in the preheated oven, one sheet at a time, for 10–12 minutes until risen and just firm to the touch. Cool for 5 minutes then, using a palette knife, transfer to a wire rack to cool completely.

4 For the filling, place the butter and peanut butter in a bowl and beat with a hand-held electric mixer for 5 minutes until pale and fluffy. Gradually beat in the icing sugar until smooth.

5 To assemble, spread or pipe the buttercream on the flat side of half of the cakes and top with a thin layer of jam. Top with the rest of the cakes.

Cook's Tip

REMEMBER TO SPACE THE MIXTURE WELL APART ON THE BAKING SHEETS TO ALLOW FOR SPREADING DURING COOKING.

GUAVA BARS

MAKES: 8–10
PREP: 30 MINS, PLUS COOLING
COOK: 30 MINS

THE GUAVA TREE IS NATIVE TO SOUTH AMERICA, BUT NOW IT IS ALSO GROWN IN OTHER TROPICAL REGIONS. GUAVAS HAVE A SWEET AND SOUR FLAVOUR – SLIGHTLY REMINISCENT OF PEARS OR STRAWBERRIES.

- 250 G/9 OZ PLAIN FLOUR
- 350 G/12 OZ SOFT LIGHT BROWN SUGAR
- ½ TSP BICARBONATE OF SODA
- ¼ TSP SALT
- 150 G/5½ OZ PORRIDGE OATS
- 225 G/8 OZ BUTTER, SOFTENED, PLUS EXTRA FOR GREASING
- 150 ML/5 FL OZ CLEAR HONEY

For the guava paste
- 300 ML/10 FL OZ GUAVA JUICE
- 70 G/2½ OZ GRANULATED SUGAR
- 50 G/1¼ OZ JAM SUGAR

OR 425 G/15 OZ READY-MADE GUAVA PASTE, SLICED

1 To make the guava paste, put the guava juice and granulated sugar into a saucepan and bring to the boil. Add the jam sugar and stir to combine, then pour into a flat mould and leave to cool to a firm paste.

2 Preheat the oven to 200°C/400°F/Gas Mark 6. Lightly grease a 30 x 20-cm/12 x 8-inch ovenproof dish.

3 Mix together the flour, sugar, bicarbonate of soda, salt and oats. Add the butter and rub in until the mixture resembles bread crumbs. Add the honey and mix well. Press half the crumble mixture into the prepared dish.

4 Cut the guava paste into thin strips and lay them on top of the crumble. Cover with the remaining crumble mixture and lightly press into place with a wooden spoon. Bake in the preheated oven for 30 minutes until golden brown. Remove from the oven and leave to cool in the tray.

5 Cut into strips about the size of a muesli bar and serve.

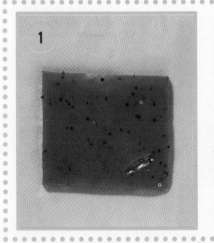

SNICKERDOODLE ICE CREAM SANDWICHES

MAKES: 8
PREP: 30 MINS, PLUS COOLING AND FREEZING
COOK: 12–14 MINS

For the ice cream

- 200 ML/7 FL OZ CANNED CONDENSED MILK
- 300 ML/10 FL OZ DOUBLE CREAM
- 1 TSP VANILLA EXTRACT
- 1 TSP GROUND CINNAMON
- 200 G/7 OZ CANNED PUMPKIN PURÉE

For the cookies

- 115 G/4 OZ BUTTER, SOFTENED
- 115 G/4 OZ CASTER SUGAR
- 1 EGG, BEATEN
- ½ TSP VANILLA EXTRACT
- 200 G/7 OZ PLAIN FLOUR
- 1½ TSP BAKING POWDER
- 1 TBSP GRANULATED SUGAR
- 2 TSP GROUND CINNAMON

THESE CINNAMON-COATED COOKIES SANDWICHED TOGETHER WITH A SWEET, SPICED PUMPKIN ICE CREAM MAKE THE PERFECT PREPARE-AHEAD PARTY DESSERT. FOR AN EXTRA TREAT, ROLL THE EDGE OF THE ICE CREAM IN CRUSHED PECAN NUTS.

1 To make the ice cream, put the condensed milk, cream and vanilla extract into a large bowl. Using a hand-held electric mixer, whisk until it holds firm peaks. Fold in the cinnamon and pumpkin purée. Spoon into a shallow freezer-proof container. Cover and freeze overnight until solid.

2 To make the cookies, preheat the oven to 180°C/350°F/Gas Mark 4. Line two large baking sheets with baking paper.

3 Put the butter and caster sugar into a large bowl and beat together until pale and creamy. Gradually beat in the egg and vanilla extract. Sift together the flour and baking powder into the bowl and stir to make a fairly stiff dough.

4 Mix together the granulated sugar and cinnamon on a flat plate. Divide the cookie dough into 16 pieces and shape each piece into a ball. Roll the balls in the cinnamon sugar, then place on the prepared baking sheets. Use your fingertips to flatten each ball to a 6-cm/2½-inch round. Sprinkle over any remaining cinnamon sugar.

5 Bake in the preheated oven for 12–14 minutes, or until golden. Leave to cool on the baking sheets for 5 minutes, then transfer to a wire rack to cool completely.

6 To assemble, remove the ice cream from the freezer and leave to stand for about 30 minutes, or until soft enough to scoop. Sandwich pairs of cookies together with a large scoop of the ice cream in between and serve immediately.

Cook's Tip

THE SANDWICHED COOKIES CAN BE FROZEN FOR UP TO 1 WEEK. LEAVE TO SOFTEN AT ROOM TEMPERATURE FOR 15 MINUTES BEFORE SERVING.

CHOCOLATE MINT CAKE POPS

MAKES: 26–28
PREP: 1 HR, PLUS CHILLING AND SETTING
COOK: 5 MINS

- 300 G/10½ OZ PLAIN CHOCOLATE, ROUGHLY CHOPPED
- 25 G/1 OZ UNSALTED BUTTER, SOFTENED
- 50 G/1¾ OZ HARD-BOILED MINT SWEETS
- 450 G/1 LB MILK CHOCOLATE
- 50 G/1¾ OZ MINI MARSHMALLOWS, ROUGHLY CHOPPED
- 26-28 LOLLIPOP STICKS
- CHOCOLATE SPRINKLES, TO DECORATE

THIS IS A CAKE POP VERSION OF 'ROCKY ROAD' AND IS ABOUT AS EASY TO MAKE AS IT GETS! THE MILK CHOCOLATE COATING IS DELICIOUS, BUT YOU CAN USE PLAIN CHOCOLATE INSTEAD FOR A MORE ADULT FLAVOUR.

1 Line a baking sheet with baking paper. Put the plain chocolate in a heatproof bowl, set the bowl over a saucepan of gently simmering water and heat until melted. Stir in the butter. Leave until the mixture is cool but not beginning to set.

2 Put the mint sweets in a polythene bag and tap firmly with a rolling pin until they are broken into tiny pieces. Finely chop 150 g/5½ oz of the milk chocolate, then stir it into the melted plain chocolate with the mints and marshmallows until thoroughly mixed.

3 As soon as the mixture is firm enough to hold its shape, roll into walnut-sized balls. Place them on the baking sheet and chill for 30–60 minutes in the refrigerator, until firm but not brittle. Push a lollipop stick into each cake ball, then chill for 10 minutes.

4 Roughly chop the remaining milk chocolate and place in a heatproof bowl set over a saucepan of simmering water and heat until melted. Remove from the heat and allow to cool a little. Dip a cake pop into the chocolate, turning it until coated. Lift it from the bowl, letting the excess drip back into the bowl, and place it in a cup or tumbler. Decorate with chocolate sprinkles. Repeat with the remaining cake pops. Chill or leave in a cool place until the chocolate has set before serving.

Cook's Tip

THESE CAKE POPS ARE PERFECT FOR CHILDREN'S BIRTHDAY PARTIES. VARY THE DECORATION BY USING SHIMMER HUNDREDS AND THOUSANDS OR COLOURFUL NONPAREILS.

ORANGE BLOSSOM AND PISTACHIO FRIANDS

MAKES: 8
PREP: 15 MINS
COOK: 15–18 MINS

THESE LIGHT-AS-AIR OVAL CAKES HAVE A NUTTY FLAVOUR WITH AN ADDED HINT OF CITRUS FROM THE ORANGE BLOSSOM WATER. THEY TASTE AMAZING WARM FROM THE OVEN BUT ARE JUST AS DELICIOUS SERVED COLD WITH A LIGHT DUSTING OF ICING SUGAR.

- 115 G/4 OZ UNSALTED BUTTER, PLUS EXTRA FOR GREASING
- 70 G/2½ OZ PISTACHIO NUTS
- 55 G/2 OZ PLAIN FLOUR
- 150 G/5½ OZ ICING SUGAR, PLUS EXTRA FOR DUSTING
- 55 G/2 OZ GROUND ALMONDS
- 3 LARGE EGG WHITES
- 2 TSP ORANGE BLOSSOM WATER
- PINCH OF SALT

1 Preheat the oven to 200°C/400°F/Gas Mark 6. Thoroughly grease an 8-hole silicone friand mould, then place the mould on a baking sheet.

2 Melt the butter in a small saucepan, then set aside to cool for 10 minutes. Put 55 g/2 oz of the pistachio nuts into a food processor or blender and process until finely ground. Roughly chop the remaining nuts and set aside.

3 Sift together the flour and sugar into a large bowl and stir in the ground pistachio nuts and ground almonds. Put the egg whites, orange blossom water and salt into a large, grease-free bowl and, using a hand-held electric mixer, beat for 1–2 minutes until foamy and floppy, but not stiff.

4 Pour the egg whites and melted butter into the dry ingredients and mix well to form a thick batter. Spoon the batter evenly into the prepared mould and scatter over the reserved pistachio nuts.

5 Bake in the preheated oven for 15–18 minutes, or until golden and just firm to the touch. Leave to cool in the mould for 2–3 minutes, then carefully turn out onto a wire rack to cool completely. Serve dusted with icing sugar, if using.

Cook's Tip

IF ORANGE BLOSSOM WATER IS UNAVAILABLE, ADD THE FINELY GRATED ZEST OF ONE SMALL ORANGE TO THE MIXTURE, OR 2 TEASPOONS ROSEWATER INSTEAD.

CHOCOLATE 'ICE-CREAM' CONES

MAKES: 16
PREP: 40 MINS, PLUS CHILLING AND SETTING
COOK: 10 MINS

THESE MINI CHOCOLATE CONES ARE FILLED WITH A DELICIOUS CHOCOLATE MOUSSE AND TOPPED WITH SWIRLS OF WHIPPED CREAM. UNLIKE REGULAR ICE CREAMS, THEY WON'T MELT IF LEFT OUT OF THE FREEZER!

- 125 G/4½ OZ MILK CHOCOLATE, ROUGHLY CHOPPED
- 200 ML/7 FL OZ DOUBLE CREAM
- 2 TBSP VANILLA SUGAR
- CHOCOLATE AND RAINBOW SUGAR SPRINKLES, TO DECORATE

For the mousse
- 200 G/7 OZ PLAIN CHOCOLATE, ROUGHLY CHOPPED
- 4 TBSP WATER
- 2 EGG WHITES
- 25 G/1 OZ CASTER SUGAR

1 Line a baking sheet with baking paper. To shape the cones, cut 16 circles of baking paper using an 18-cm/7-inch plate as a guide. Fold the circles in half and then cut them in half just to one side of the fold. Shape each semi-circle into a cone so the straight edges meet to create a cone of double-thickness paper, securing it in place with sticky tape.

2 Put the milk chocolate in a heatproof bowl set over a saucepan of gently simmering water and heat until melted. Place a teaspoon of melted chocolate into a cone so that it's about a third full and spread the chocolate up the sides using a pastry brush. Repeat with the remaining cones. Invert them onto the baking sheet and chill for at least 30 minutes, until set.

3 To make the mousse, put the plain chocolate and water in a heatproof bowl set over a saucepan of gently simmering water and heat until melted. Whisk the egg whites in another clean mixing bowl to soft peaks. Whisk in the caster sugar, a little at a time. Tip the melted chocolate onto the egg whites and fold together with a spatula. Stand the cones up in glasses or a small bowl and carefully spoon in the mousse. Chill in the refrigerator for 1 hour.

4 Whip the cream with the vanilla sugar until only just peaking. Put it into a small piping bag fitted with a 1-cm/½-inch star nozzle. Peel the paper from the cones and pipe swirls of cream on top. Scatter with sprinkles and serve immediately.

Cook's Tip
TRY TOPPING THESE CONES WITH FRESH RASPBERRIES INSTEAD OF THE WHIPPED CREAM AND GRATE OVER SOME WHITE CHOCOLATE CURLS JUST BEFORE SERVING.

BLUEBERRY CHEESECAKE BARS

MAKES: 12
PREP: 30 MINS, PLUS COOLING AND CHILLING
COOK: 50–55 MINS

- 200 G/7 OZ DIGESTIVE BISCUITS, CRUSHED
- 70 G/2½ OZ BUTTER, MELTED, PLUS EXTRA FOR GREASING
- 175 G/6 OZ BLUEBERRIES
- 450 G/1 LB FULL-FAT SOFT CHEESE
- ½ TSP VANILLA EXTRACT
- 150 G/5½ OZ CASTER SUGAR
- 3 EGGS, BEATEN
- 150 ML/5 FL OZ SOURED CREAM
- 1 TBSP CORNFLOUR

CHEESECAKE IS ALWAYS A REAL CROWD-PLEASER AND THIS ONE, FLAVOURED WITH VANILLA AND FRESH BLUEBERRIES, IS NO EXCEPTION! YOU CAN MAKE IT UP TO A DAY IN ADVANCE BUT REMOVE IT FROM THE REFRIGERATOR ABOUT 30 MINUTES BEFORE SERVING.

1 Preheat the oven to 150°C/300°F/Gas Mark 2. Grease a 28 x 18-cm/ 11 x 7-inch traybake tin and line with baking paper. Put the crushed biscuits into a bowl and stir in the melted butter. Press into the base of the prepared tin, levelling smooth with the back of a spoon. Chill in the refrigerator for 10–15 minutes.

2 Purée half the blueberries in a blender or food processor and set aside. Put the soft cheese, vanilla extract and sugar into a large bowl and beat with a wooden spoon until smooth. Gradually beat in the eggs, then fold in the soured cream and cornflour.

3 Scatter the remaining blueberries over the biscuit base, then spoon over the cheesecake mixture and gently level the surface with a spatula. Drop small spoonfuls of the reserved blueberry purée over the mixture, then drag the tip of a knife through the mixture to create a rippled effect.

4 Bake in the preheated oven for 50–55 minutes, or until just set. Turn off the oven and leave the cheesecake inside until cold, then transfer to the refrigerator and chill for 2–3 hours. To serve, carefully remove from the tin and cut into bars.

Cook's Tip

REPLACE THE WHOLE BLUEBERRIES WITH 85 G/3 OZ CHOCOLATE CHIPS AND TOP THE BARS WITH SPOONS OF WARMED CHOCOLATE AND HAZELNUT SPREAD INSTEAD OF THE FRUIT PURÉE.

PISTACHIO AND ALMOND TUILES

MAKES: 6
PREP: 30 MINS, PLUS COOLING
COOK: 10–15 MINS

THESE FEATHER-LIGHT BISCUITS MAKE A LOVELY TEA-TIME TREAT OR THEY CAN BE SERVED ON TOP OF ICE CREAM TO ADD TEXTURE TO A DESSERT.

- 1 EGG WHITE
- 55 G/2 OZ GOLDEN CASTER SUGAR
- 25 G/1 OZ PLAIN FLOUR
- 25 G/1 OZ PISTACHIO NUTS, FINELY CHOPPED
- 25 G/1 OZ GROUND ALMONDS
- ½ TSP ALMOND EXTRACT
- 40 G/1½ OZ UNSALTED BUTTER, MELTED AND COOLED

1 Preheat the oven to 160°C/325°F/Gas Mark 3. Line two baking sheets with baking paper.

2 Whisk the egg white lightly with the sugar, then stir in the flour, pistachio nuts, ground almonds, almond extract and butter, mixing to a soft paste.

3 Place walnut-sized spoonfuls of the mixture on the prepared baking sheets and use the back of the spoon to spread as thinly as possible. Bake in the preheated oven for 10–15 minutes, until pale golden.

4 Quickly lift each biscuit with a palette knife and place over the side of a rolling pin while still warm to shape into a curve. When set, transfer to a wire rack to cool completely before serving.

Cook's Tip
TO GET SUPER-THIN TUILES, SPREAD THE MIXTURE DIRECTLY ONTO SILICONE BAKING SHEETS WITH A PALETTE KNIFE.

INDEX